T0128743

Servitude of the Church

Servitude of the Church

A Pocket Guide to Developing
a Servant's Heart

Willie Jenkins

SERVITUDE OF THE CHURCH
A POCKET GUIDE TO DEVELOPING A SERVANT'S HEART

iUniverse books may be ordered through booksellers or by contacting:

iUniverse
1663 Liberty Drive
Bloomington, IN 47403
www.iuniverse.com
1-800-Authors (1-800-288-4677)

ISBN: 978-1-4917-7955-2 (sc)
ISBN: 978-1-4917-7954-5 (e)

Library of Congress Control Number: 2015916539

Print information available on the last page.

iUniverse rev. date: 01/31/2017

Scripture taken from the King James Version of the Bible.

Contents

I would like to dedicate this book to my beautiful new wife, Kimberly; you are a constant source of love and inspiration. Because of you, I found the strength to dust off this manuscript and give it legs to walk. Additionally, I dedicate this book to all my amazing kids: Willie, Kashion, Dante, Tommy, Cruz, and Jewelia. I pray unceasingly for each of you. May you each read this book and discover your own servant's heart. My greatest hope is that reading this book will forever impact your lives and that your hearts will always remain receptive to what God desires to do in and through you.

Preface

This book has its origin in a turn of events that might seem unusual if you are not accustomed to experiencing the strange ways in which God sometimes tries to hand us His blessings. Well, as my story goes, I found myself fervently praying to God for a financial miracle to manifest in my life to address some pressing needs I had back in August 2005. While I was ensnared by the despair of my depressing circumstances, my pastor shared a particular message with me concerning how God often gives him strange and bizarre instructions in order to deliver him from difficulty. However, God gives the message to him only after he has obeyed certain basic initial guidance. As was my practice back then, I lived with a constant daily expectation that God would turn my situation around instantaneously by giving me a sudden financial miracle out of nowhere. I was naive back then; now I know that I should have been asking God for a financial harvest based on seeds I had previously sown. On the evening of August 14, I prayed to God for answers before going to bed.

The next day, on the morning of August 15, 2005, Savaslas Lofton, one of the ministers from my church, pulled me aside and said, "Brother Willie, you need to write a book on servitude of the church." I must admit that his statement astonished me because it was directly in line with my plea to God from the night before. The coincidence, as the saying goes, hit me like a ton of bricks. While I might have been hoping someone would just hand me some Benjamins, Minister Lofton gave me, in an instant, all that I truly needed in order to turn my situation around. Right then and there, I realized that I already had the treasures I needed for my deliverance. In fact, God had placed them in me at birth in order to fulfill His plan for my life.

But here is my point. As far as submission goes, I remember that some time ago, I told Minister Lofton I would submit myself to his spiritual leadership, correction and discipline included. Guess what? God has a strange sense of humor, and He arranged it so that I would have to listen to and adhere to

Minister Lofton's guidance in order to receive the miraculous blessing God had in store for me. This, my friend, is how this first book came about. Staying true to my original instructions, I have titled my book *Servitude of the Church: A Pocket Guide to Developing a Servant's Heart.*

Acknowledgments

I would like to give a special shout-out to several individuals who have been instrumental in my spiritual and professional development over the past fourteen years. God has used you all in various ways to minister to me at key moments when I needed encouragement most. I love you all dearly.

Bishop Dr. Mikel Brown, thank you for being my spiritual father. God knew the guidance I needed, and He led me to you. Thank you for taking on the monumental task of putting me on the path that leads to greatness. I needed you then, and I need you now. So I guess you're stuck with me.

First Lady Debra Brown, thank you for being an amazing spiritual mom to me over the years and for being a super spiritual grand-godmother to my children.

Minister Savaslas Lofton, thank you for the idea and title of this book, which you gave to me back on August 15, 2005, at around nine thirty in the morning. What you freely gave, I took and am now running with.

Elder Lyndon Mayfield, thank you for always being a true example of what it means to serve and for remaining vigilant while on your various duty posts in God's kingdom.

Pastor Scott, thank you for your constant encouragement and for always being willing to share with me your thought-provoking biblical wisdom and insights.

Elder Bill Smith, thank you for being there when I needed guidance, nuggets, and a swift kick in the behind, whether or not you knew that was what you were providing at the time.

Elder Reggie Mainor, thank you for your silent courage, which has been a major rallying point for countless men in our ministry.

Elder Lavonne Nelson, thank you for being a breath of fresh air in providing a much-needed atmosphere of loving discipline and professionalism that always demanded my best.

Elder Charles Newman, thank you for being a steady pillar that I can look up to in the church and for putting your trust in my VA benefits consulting business when, at times, few people did.

I also want to thank the rest of the Christian Joy Center (CJC) family and friends for showing me the consistent love of Christ.

Chapter 1

Understanding Your Call to Serve

On Monday, August 15, 2005, around ten thirty at night, I embarked upon the somewhat formidable journey of finishing this book. I had noticed God's calling on my life approximately two to three years before. I had no choice but to accept it; there was no alternative for me. For the first time in my life, I realized I had to get busy, get basic, and get bold when it came to submitting to church leadership. That meant I had to submit myself fully to the pastor and other leaders of the church. The moment I committed to doing that, the Lord began to pour into my life in a profound way. I started receiving a tremendous outpouring of wise counsel from my pastor. Additionally, I made it a point to be at church every day, which I truly believe was responsible for saving my life and keeping me here to this day.

When I first began volunteering at church prior to my commitment to becoming a servant, I had a small inkling of what God wanted me to do, although the details were not clear to me. I believe we all have instinctive knowledge that God has a greater purpose for our lives, even if we are not currently operating in that calling. I have come to realize that the key to discovering what God desires for us to accomplish on earth is to get busy serving in some area of the ministry, whether or not that service directly has anything to do with your designed purpose. The key is to get busy serving in some capacity in God's house. I understand that I could only identify God's master plan for my life by submitting to His development process and humbling myself to the point where it hurt at times and was extremely uncomfortable most of the time. There were many days when I would get to church and not feel like cleaning up, waxing floors, pulling weeds, mopping, and doing other such janitorial duties. Despite how I felt, I chose to surrender to God's plan and pitch in wherever I was needed. I would assist the church's administrative staff with their workload as well.

If you remember nothing else after reading this book, please keep close to your heart what I am about to say next. Self-sacrifice is crucial to developing the type of servant's heart that captures God's attention and gets His blessings flowing in your direction. Did you get that? I call this trademark quality servant self-sacrifice.

My pastor once referred to me as a volunteer when he saw me laboring around the church. Then and there, out of nowhere, I summoned the courage to correct him by saying, "I am a servant, and the difference is that a volunteer will put limits on the amount of time he is willing to give. However, servants are different because they can't go anywhere as long as there is work to be done around the church. Our labor is not for the eyes of men." I was not sure where those words came from, because I never had needed to or felt it proper to correct anything my pastor said. I respect him, and I trust that God gives him powerful words of encouragement and insights into the lives of his church members. Therefore, correcting him was not a common practice for me. That day, I wanted him to see that I brought to the table a servant's heart rather than a volunteer's mentality.

But let me tell you something: experiencing a breakthrough after serving in the church all day long is sweet, especially when you needed one in a bad way. This particular section is near and dear to me because I had to both give up much and release a lot to God. In August 2005, I realized some counterproductive things I had been doing to myself over the previous three years, and I had to make a decision to give those things to God.

I should add here that the devil was not pleased with the spiritual progress I was making in my young Christian walk. His carefully planned, well-orchestrated attacks on my life came in many forms, but mostly in the form of negative thoughts, ideas, and suggestions. As Christian believers, we must keep in mind that Satan only comes to kill, steal, and destroy. That is his MO, plain and simple. For that reason, I had to constantly check my thoughts to guard against any jealousy that tried to surface whenever I saw my brothers and sisters receiving their breakthrough blessings. Additionally, I had to resist developing a rebellious attitude when things did not go my way or did not happen on my timetable. In every attack I experienced, I had to remember to surrender it all to God.

I wanted to be a vital part of what God was doing in the overall life of my church. I recognized the standard of excellence that permeated the place as well as the spirit of excellence that the pastor engendered throughout the ministry. Because I wanted to be part of this awesome work of God, I knew I had to be willing to submit in all areas. Do not be surprised when the Lord begins to reveal and expose things to you as a result of your humble surrender to His plan. Early in my Christian walk, God revealed to me that He is displeased with us when we show up late for church services, constantly monitor the clock for closing time, and leave early. When I became a servant in the church, God began exposing various things to me, such as scheduling, special events, fund-raising, and the importance of being led by the Holy Spirit.

I wish to end this particular chapter by stressing the importance of being properly positioned as a faithful servant in the house of the Lord, because serving is how you will begin to experience the fullness and richness of His abundant blessings as they begin to flow into your life. You cannot afford to live any other way if you desire to operate in His kingdom and enjoy His best for your life.

Chapter 2

Serving Births Your Ministry

Waiting on your God-ordained ministry is key. It is important to realize that waiting does not imply being inactive or doing nothing, as I have come to learn through the teachings of my pastor, Dr. Mikel Brown. Moreover, waiting on your ministry is biblical, and you will see throughout the Bible that it is a process that occurs in stages. Only after I made the decision to submit to my pastor and his delegated leadership did the Lord begin revealing and unveiling specific things to me through prophetic words I received after submitting to God's plan for my life.

For instance, I vividly remember when prophet David Guy came to Christian Joy Center (CJC) in 2002. He told me that the Lord had spoken to him the night before about me and that

I would be doing something special for the Lord. Also, earlier that same year, apostle Turnel Nelson spoke a specific prophecy into my life, telling me I would be extremely wealthy around March or April 2005. The prophecies of these two mighty men of God went hand in hand with the numerous prophetic words that my pastor and spiritual father, Dr. Brown, had already been speaking into my life.

Because of the many prophetic words that others have spoken over my life, I have come under intense spiritual warfare, because the devil does not want those prophetic utterances to come to pass. In fact, Satan's attacks intensified around the time I began writing this book. That defeated foe was simply trying to prevent this best seller from reaching bookstores. As with the apostle Paul's encouragement to young Timothy in 1 Timothy 1:18, which states, "This charge I commit unto thee, son Timothy, according to the prophecies which went before on thee, that thou by them mightest war a good warfare" (KJV), I too found myself having to contend for the faith in order to safeguard the prophetic utterances entrusted to me.

Additionally, I found that in times of great distress and spiritual warfare, the following two verses from 1 Timothy were also powerful scriptures that provided strength and reassurance throughout my ordeals: "O Timothy, keep that which is committed to thy trust, avoiding profane and vain babblings, and oppositions of science falsely so called" (1 Timothy 6:20 KJV) and "Neglect not the gift that is in thee, which was given thee by prophecy, with the laying on of the hands of the presbytery" (1 Timothy 4:14 KJV).

This is why it is crucial to listen to your man of God, because he truly does have in his mouth the Word of God for your life, which is designed to take you to your proper destination in life. Have I always listened to him the way that I should have? No. Should I have? Yes. Did I suffer unnecessarily as a result of my unwillingness to heed his instructions? Yes. However, whenever I failed to say yes to God's directions, I found that God's grace and mercy were sufficient to save me from my foolishness. Indeed, God is patient, merciful, and kind.

Do you really want to know what it is all about? It is about taking care of the church, which boils down to the people. After all, it is all about establishing the kingdom of God here on earth. We do that by building and adding to the church one soul at a time. It is important to note that everyone in the body of Christ, no matter how significant or insignificant one's role seems to be, has a vital role to play in achieving God's overall mandate for His church. The apostle Paul said it this way in 1 Corinthians 12:22–25:

> Nay, much more those members of the body, which seem to be more feeble, are necessary: And those members of the body, which we think to be less honourable, upon these we bestow more abundant honour; and our uncomely parts have more abundant comeliness. For our comely pars have no need: but God hath tempered the body together, having given more abundant honour to that part which lacked: That there should be no schism in the body; but that the members should have the same care one for another.

So you see—we all have an important part to play in accomplishing God's work here on earth. But we need to keep in mind that every part of the body of Christ needs to be submitted to God-ordained leadership, or else you are not covered. You must surrender your gifts, talents, and abilities to the leader who has spiritual charge over you.

Feelings and emotions should not ever get in the way of you submitting to the person whom God has chosen to lead, develop, and guide you, because that individual is in your life to bring you to a place of maturity in Christ. Humble submission to proper church leadership keeps us in fellowship with our heavenly Father, and it helps us to remain guarded by the protective covering of a spiritual leader.

Additionally, we must remain in humble submission to church leadership so as not to give the devil a foothold in our lives and so that we are in position for our calling and spiritual gifts to be properly deployed for the glory of God's kingdom. Consider the great statesman Nehemiah. God impressed upon him to rebuild the walls of Jerusalem because they were in such a terrible state of dilapidation and ruin. Despite the tremendous opposition he and his countrymen encountered in obeying God's instructions, he remained steadfast in his determination to repair those walls to their former state of glory. Because of the people's commitment to the task, they were able to complete the task in only fifty-two days by working day and night with their weapons in one hand and their tools in the other. Even when Nehemiah was tempted to leave the work to address petty issues and problems that certain foreigners were causing, he chose to remain on task and not come down off the wall. Throughout the entire wall-building ordeal, Nehemiah remained in humble servitude to God's rebuilding plan.

As further illustration of how we should be in constant servitude to God-sent leaders, examine the relationship between the prophet Elijah and his ever-faithful servant, Elisha. Elisha served Elijah faithfully for many years before receiving his prophetic anointing through the mantle that fell from Elijah's hand when his chariot was taken up in a whirlwind. The point we need to understand is that Elisha's faithful submission to Elijah is the thing that qualified him to be elevated to his position as the next premier prophet on the scene in the Northern Kingdom of Israel when the time came. For his faithful service to the man of God, Elisha received a double-portion blessing of prophetic anointing.

So you can clearly see that faithfully serving the leader God has appointed to lead you is the key to one day moving forward in your divine appointment. Whereas I once had a volunteer's mentality when it came to serving, I now glorify the Lord by approaching His business with a servant's mind-set. This I now do only by the grace of God. I am grateful for everything God has done in my life and for all the messes He has delivered me from. He truly has blessed me exceedingly and abundantly above all that I ever hoped to accomplish in life. Luke said it best when he stated,

> But he that knew not, and did commit things worthy of stripes, shall be beaten with few stripes. For unto whomsoever much is given, of him shall be much required: and to whom men have committed much, of him they will ask the more. (Luke 12:48 KJV)

Because I recognize that God has done so much for me, I feel I owe Him a huge debt of gratitude—repayment I can demonstrate only in the level of my surrender to Him. This is why I know I have to be willing and obedient and to do things I ordinarily wouldn't do and allow God to stretch me in ways that are oftentimes uncomfortable.

Years ago, I prayed to be a faithful servant in God's kingdom. God revealed to me one day that I would indeed become a servant and would be called upon to submit even to those individuals following behind me, despite the fact that in many instances, I would be a leader to them. So be careful what you pray for, because it more than likely will come true when you are earnestly praying for God's will to be done.

Remember—God does have a sense of humor. He does answer our prayers, but His responses rarely resemble what we were anticipating. Rest assured, however, His solutions are always best.

Chapter 3

Servitude without Obedience Is Impossible

One thing I have come to realize is that I am right where God wants me to be; I am situated in the middle of His divine will for my life. This realization suddenly dawned on me at some point near the end of 2001 or beginning of 2002. Prior to arriving at this place of peace and contentment with God's plan for my life, I went through several well-orchestrated spiritual attacks from the enemy. However, I did not recognize them as such at the time. I figured that those ordeals were simply part of the normal, everyday struggles we all encounter. What can I say? I was an integral part of Satan's kingdom back then. I chalked my bad fortunes up to reaping what I had been sowing for so many years.

But God's timing is impeccable. While I was going through some difficult struggles, a coworker approached me out of the blue and invited me to visit his church, Christian Joy Center. While that individual is no longer part of CJC, I took him up on his offer to attend a service, and I have been there ever since. It is the place where God met me, saved me, and delivered me from many things that were destroying my life. I arrived at CJC with mental, physical, and spiritual baggage in tow. I arrived at the doorstep of this awesome ministry at the moment when it seemed I was reaping the negative consequences of all the bad seeds I had ever sown in life. Shortly after my arrival, however, I knew that my being there was all part of God's plan.

The Lord truly does work in mysterious ways. That coworker pestered me about visiting his church. He would not let up. Each time he invited me, I would make one excuse after another. However, exactly eleven days prior to the 9/11 terrorist attack on the World Trade Center, I got laid off from the great job I had at the time with Raytheon. The layoff caused me to do a great deal of soul searching for answers. I wondered, *Why me? And what should I do next?* In actuality, I knew the reason for my being let go. Around that time, I had sustained an on-the-job injury that I'd failed to report. The day after the injury, I'd violated company protocol by going to the clinic without reporting the incident. So when layoff time came around, my name was on the list of individuals to be let go.

After that incident, I vowed that I would never work like that for any business again. Whenever I attended the CJC church services, I paid close attention to everything the pastor ministered from the pulpit. For some reason, I was always fascinated by the messages he taught about becoming self-employed and starting a business of your own. I even attempted to land employment at the church; however, my heart was not right at the time. I was attending Western Technical Institute in El Paso, Texas, at that time. Prior to graduating from WTI, I owned and operated three businesses, so it is apparent that the entrepreneurial spirit was alive in me, and that was the reason I was so captivated by Pastor Brown's messages on self-reliance through entrepreneurship.

I vividly remember prophetic words I got from my pastor indicating that the business I was running at the time was being operated based on a flawed business concept and with a lack of business acumen. I immediately shut down the entire business venture by closing bank accounts, releasing DBAs, allowing company registrations to expire, and turning over my business leads to someone else. Around 2002, I started to get serious about the Lord, and I became more focused on knowing God's call on my life. I realized then that I had only one option in life: to start being more obedient and willing to humble myself by the grace of God. The Lord has entrusted me with the responsibility of accomplishing many things in a short time. Therefore, I am familiar with the phrase I quoted earlier from Luke 12:48, which informs us, "to whom much is given, of him shall be much required." Beyond a shadow of a doubt, I know that God keeps me, and I am convinced He kept me even when I was deep in my past sins.

The Lord put in me a heart to serve—one that is totally surrendered and obedient to God at all costs. That also means being submitted to my pastor and to his ordained leadership. Have I always felt that way? No. Has anybody ever made me mad? Yes. Did it matter? No. Did I ever harbor any negative thoughts, ideas, or suggestions at times in my serving? Yes.

But as a result of my surrender to God and not my feelings, I was always determined to cast down any thought that tried to exalt itself against my knowledge of God's will for my life so that I would at all times be free to serve Him without guilt or shame. Have I always known that? No. Do I know it now? Yes!

Once, while talking to one of the elders from my church about a particular issue, the more we talked, I could tell he sensed I was getting mad or at least a little irritated by what he was saying. He asked me about the incident later, and I told him that yes, I had gotten a little bit ruffled by his comments but that in the long run, it did not matter what I thought or felt. I told him the only thing that mattered was that I had been given an order to carry out. Furthermore, I indicated that doing God's will and taking care of the upkeep of His house were my only concerns.

Submission, obedience, and servitude have nothing to do with your personal thoughts, feelings, concerns, and dislikes. True submission must be rendered in all situations, because it is, after all, about Jesus and acting in his perfect will, not his permissive will. For this reason, the Lord revealed to me the ABCs of servitude and obedience to Him and His appointed leaders. Becoming a true servant of God comes with a price that you can either pay now or later—but the price will be higher later. I chose to pay now rather than later by submitting wholeheartedly to the entire servant-building process from *A* to *Z*. You can too; it's easier than you might think.

One key thing we all should understand is that God blesses obedience, and He curses disobedience. Had I not by the grace of God started to get busy serving the Lord by being faithful, the abundance that I now enjoy would never have manifested in my life. This is why I am always sowing my seeds in at least seven to eight different places at any given time. Who knows when God will decide to return to me a bountiful harvest on any one of those seeds? God's blessings, needless to say, always show up in our lives at just the right moment.

When I was involved with a particular business organization, I once had the opportunity to serve a millionaire and his wife. He gave me some useful financial advice that I took and ran with. In fact, his advice encouraged me to get my Texas loan-officer license in order to begin working with a local mortgage company. The Lord made it possible for me to serve faithfully there in another man's businesses. Check out what the book of Luke has to say about being faithful over another man's affairs:

> He that is faithful in that which is least is faithful also in much: and he that is unjust in the least is unjust also in much. If therefore ye have not been faithful in the unrighteous mammon, who will commit to your trust the true riches? And if you have not been faithful in that which is another man's, who shall give you that which is your own? (Luke 16:10–12 KJV)

Did you catch what the writer said in the twelfth verse? The implication is that you must prove yourself as a faithful steward over someone else's affairs before God gives you that which is truly your own. Grasping this spiritual truth is vital to receiving His best for your life. This is why servitude is so crucial to fulfilling the purpose God has for you, as well as for Him giving you the wherewithal to complete your assignment here on earth.

When serving, it is important to surrender all, because God covers us through His grace and mercy. Some might say it takes a lot of time to develop a servant's heart. However, it is possible, because in Christ, all things are possible: "But Jesus beheld them, and said unto them, With men this is impossible; but with God all things are possible" (Matthew 19:26 KJV).

So there you have it. Jesus himself tells us emphatically that all things are possible whenever we put our trust in God. It is important that we keep this in mind. I did not always feel like serving with a cheerful heart; I can recall times when I went to work in the church while wearing all my anguish, hurt, and anxiety on my face. Without fail, however, God would send Holy Spirit–directed church staff members to give me a timely encouraging word. Whether you are called upon to throw out the trash, pick up paper, sweep and mop latrines, or vacuum the sanctuary, the Lord will provide you with all the strength and encouragement you need once you make the commitment to get on board with His program and surrender your will to Him.

Around the time when God was transforming me from a self-willed, stubborn individual into a servant He could call upon at any time, He revealed to me that serving has nothing to do with you or the people you are called upon to serve.

Rather, it is all about carrying out God's business, plain and simple. Once you have caught the vision of your church as revealed through the pastor, you must do your part in every way to ensure that vision comes to pass. After all, the corporate vision of your church is designed to be of immeasurable benefit to you and your entire family. Therefore, do all you can to assist your pastor in making the spiritual vision an earthly reality.

We should not become so engrossed in the affairs of this world that we neglect to tend to the affairs of God's kingdom. This type of neglect is a great injustice that too many Christians are guilty of committing. Please do not allow this to be an offense that the Lord can charge to your account. We should only be concerned with pleasing Him. When we wholeheartedly commit our service to God in this manner, we then stand on the front lines, ensuring that the gospel message can be spread as God intended.

Chapter 4

Serving amid Misfortune

Everything you have read up to this point should tell you that God had to deliver me from a lot of issues. No doubt I traveled through life carrying an enormous amount of self-condemnation and guilt for the things I did prior to God rescuing me. For many years, I was paralyzed both mentally and spiritually, always haunted by recurring thoughts of things I did in my past that knowingly and unknowingly hurt many in my family. All I can say to that shameful past is that God's grace and mercy are good, because they delivered me from certain wrath I was not prepared to face. To this day, I rely on God to keep me. This is my constant prayer, because I know the depths He had to reach in order to pull me out of the pit of despair. I depend on Him alone to keep me from falling, and that is why I have no other choice but to serve the Lord with my whole heart. Nowadays, this is my greatest joy.

It is funny when I stop to think about the mind-set I had many years ago. If anyone in my former life would have told me then that there would come a day when I would be working in the church on my free time without getting paid to do so, I would have shared a few choice words and then told that individual to quit smoking crack. Back then, the thought of being a servant for God, let alone anyone else, was the furthest thing from my mind. My life was all about me and what I could get out of the deal.

Looking back on everything I have been through, I believe beyond a shadow of a doubt that the redemption of my life will be used in the ministry for someone's breakthrough testimony of God's amazing deliverance. It is my hope that my life story will encourage many to receive Jesus Christ as their Lord and Savior. Because of Christ, I live each day to make a profound difference in the lives of others. The thing that keeps me grounded is the sobering truth that Jesus suffered unimaginable suffering for my sake and yours. I live my life now knowing that life is all about presenting His story and not mine. He paid the ultimate sacrifice so that I could have a second chance at life. Everything I now do for the Lord pales in comparison to what He did on the cross for me nearly two thousand years ago.

That is why I pray and believe this book will be a blessing to all who read it. I want people to realize that Jesus is bigger than the current circumstances they are experiencing. My message in this book applies especially to those faithful church workers who labor tirelessly to ensure that the ministry can function seamlessly during service times, including the security personnel, greeters, ushers, bookstore personnel, outreach team members, nursery and children's church workers, audiovisual personnel, choir, and praise-and-worship team members, as well as the countless other Ministry of Helps support personnel. Keep in mind that your service to God is not about you; therefore, serve with joy. Remember that as servants in the church we must present ourselves in the best light possible. We do this by relying on God's strength and not our own to serve others. More often than not, your service will touch the lives of people battling suicidal thoughts, rape, depression, and a host of other oppressive conditions.

In order to step into the proper frame of mind as a servant, you should wake up each day relying on the Holy Spirit to lead you in the area of servitude. You must maintain this focus from the time you pull into the parking of the church until the time the last person departs the church grounds and you close out your duties. At all times, listen carefully to the directives and instructions your leaders provide. It is important to understand that the more we are in sync with what God demands from us in the way of serving, the more our service frees the church leaders to do what they were called to do. They are then free to minister unhindered to the needs of church members and visitors.

Always be on the lookout for ways you can take initiative to make the job of everyone around you easier. Pick up after yourself, and always police your areas of responsibility to ensure they are in a high state of cleanliness and serviceability. Survey both inside and outside the church, and remain vigilant so that you can notice issues that need to be addressed or corrected. By being proactive and addressing issues on the spot, you intervene to ensure that neither the pastor nor any of his other leaders need to involve themselves in matters that do not require their attention. I can assure you that your leaders will greatly appreciate your thoughtfulness and attention to detail.

In everything you do, remember to serve with a spirit of excellence. God will certainly reward your faithful service to his people.

Chapter 5

When You Serve, Others Will Notice

One particular day, when I was feeling down in the dumps and somewhat unworthy, I approached one of the CJC elders and asked him what he felt others saw in me that would give me hope that I had something of value to offer anyone. He simply said, "People see the glory of the Lord on your life." He further added, "It is not up to you to assess your own value and worth. Once you allow Him entry into your heart, it is then God's responsibility to simply shine through you." When God is able to freely work through your life, others will be able to see His handiwork present in your life, both in and out of season.

That elder was referring to the Shechinah glory that manifests mightily whenever we find ourselves in the presence of God, as Moses experienced when God appeared to him to give him the Ten Commandments. The Shechinah glory represents the visible manifestation of God's presence. When we come out of the presence of the Shechinah glory, people will recognize a certain glow and illumination all over us. This glory illuminates people when they are witnessing or evangelizing for the Lord.

For example, if there is a problem of sin in the church, then it will be next to impossible for the Holy Spirit to manifest in that unwelcoming atmosphere. The Holy Spirit will not manifest in environments where He is not welcome. For this reason, it is crucial that we freely yield the right of way to the Holy Spirit so that He can reign supreme in every area of our lives. However, when we repent of the sinful wrongdoing, the atmosphere then becomes conducive to the free-flowing power of the Holy Spirit. As we mature in Christ and begin to sin less, we will experience God's Shechinah glory on a more regular basis.

But this powerful flow of God's presence is not evident when we are going through the refining process of correction. As we mature in Christ, we will experience times of falling and getting up that should point toward spiritual growth and progression in the Lord. This process will be characterized by seasons of falling, repenting, and getting up. But as we grow more in our walk with our Lord and Savior, we should arrive at a rather steady state in our relationship with Him. Therefore, we must not despise those times when our heavenly Father chooses to chasten us as a result of the sin we have allowed to enter our lives. His chastening is evidence that He is indeed our Father. Proverbs states, "My son, despise not the chastening of the Lord; neither be weary of his correction" (Proverbs 3:11 KJV).

However, God regards us as bastards when we fail to endure His correction. It is important to note that as a servant of God, you must hold yourself to a higher standard than others who might not realize they too have been called to be servants in the body of Christ.

Over the years, I have experienced many instances when I had to simply endure chastening. In one particular instance, I was derelict in the performance of a certain one of my security duties. Rather than being at my assigned post, I went forward to hold a woman's baby so that she could go to the front of the church in order to respond to an altar call. Although I figured I was doing a noble deed, I did, however, leave my security post unmanned. Needless to say, the elder over church security let me know about my lack of judgment. When he told me I would need to sit down from my responsibilities for a month, I was both sad and hurt. However, I was aware of the serious implications of my security breach, because I had not been in position to perform my duties if anything of a serious nature had occurred. Again, I had to chalk the correction up to another learning experience and become better in the process and not bitter.

Furthermore, whether you are wrong or right, you should be willing to accept constructive criticism, rebuke, and admonishment from leadership, especially from your pastor. Taking correction is one of the hallmark signs of maturity in an individual. This is why I have resolved with everything in me to do God's will and go through everything He wants me to experience in order to be positioned right where I should be. I made a decision several years ago that I would humble myself under God's mighty hand so that He would not have the task of doing it. As a servant, my constant prayer to God is as follows:

> I submit my heart, mind, soul, and strength to You, Lord.

> I submit all my gifts, talents, abilities, and time to You, God, and to my pastor.

> I submit to being a faithful servant who tithes and faithfully gives offerings.

> I submit to being an obedient child of God.

> I submit to accepting everything according to Your perfect will, and I pray to stay in it and never stray into Your permissive will.

I pray this way because I have committed to being a person of solid character, integrity, and conviction while endeavoring never to be a person guided by preferences, as prioritizing preferences breeds compromises, contempt, complacency, confusion, and curses. Because the Lord has put a serious mandate on my life, I have no option but to live a life of conviction. I must be willing and obedient at all times; I must

Willie Jenkins

do whatever He wants and do it whenever and for however long He wants. This is now my philosophy for life.

In closing, I believe strongly that the thoughts and testimonials I have shared throughout this book have blessed you, and I hope the book has served its purpose of inspiring you to become a true servant within your local church. I would also like to encourage you to pray earnestly about becoming part of a God-inspired, biblically based church in your local community, where you can be fed on a weekly basis. On a final note, I leave you with these words (to borrow and paraphrase from a familiar JFK speech many years ago): ask not what your church can do for you but what you can do for your church—and then get busy doing it!

Notes

Printed in the United States
By Bookmasters